Russian Blue Cat as Pets

A Russian Blue Cat Care Guide

Russian Blue Facts & Information, buying, health, diet, lifespan, breeding, care and more!

By Lolly Brown

Foreword

The Russian Blue Cat is known for its innate curiosity, its outward calmness and quiet tranquility. They are lauded for being friendly and intelligent; able to create close bonds with its guardians - but always favoring one above all - and has been observed to pick up quickly on human movement; able to mimic movements like opening doors and inspecting the contents of lidded containers.

But most notable of the many great qualities of the RB is their natural instinct and sensitivity to detecting human emotions. They astound many with their keen sense of mood identification and respond to these emotional shifts and transitions in their caregivers accordingly. The RB indeed makes for a great friend and companion for any season and will be utterly loyal and loving of you and the people it comes in contact with who extend it kindness and respect.

Provide the Russian Blue a variety of toys and it will love the provisions you give and gladly show you its gratitude by including you in its playtime. They are known to develop very strong bonds with their caregivers, loved ones as well as other pets in the family.

Table of Contents

Chapter One: Introduction

Fairytale-like stories have been spun and woven to tell about the striking beauty of this majestic gem of a feline, the Russian Blue.

For as far back and long ago as when man first learnt to stand upright, build shelter and discover that food tasted better if put on fire, cats have been consistently favored animals man chose with whom to share roof and food.

Felines, of all breeds, have been transcribed in ancient texts, poems and writings. They've been immortalized in frescoes, paintings and murals. All these evidence and give us reason to believe the notion that they have been capturing human hearts for a very long time. They have been seen in ancient carvings of stone, wood and slate and marble. They also have been famously documented to have lived privileged lives in the lap of luxury, counted into many royal courts, privy to the very secrets within these walled kingdoms.

This beautifully-coated feline which comes in varying colors of shimmering silver to slightly darker shades of utterly mystifying slate grey, is the incomparable, Russian Blue. Tending to develop very close ties with their guardians, humans and caregivers, they are often sought out as animal companions and pets because of their no-fuss personalities, their unusual coat and trademark traits of cleverness, playfulness, devotion and tranquility.

For over a century their dense, short coat has been the outstanding hallmark of the Russian breed which has contributed in its popularity and why it enjoys continued fame to this day. The richly dense coat of the Russian Blue stands from its body and is thick enough for you to draw patterns on which will stay until you smooth down its fur.

Children have long discovered this quality and utilized them to send "messages" to other people they live with at home.

Read on to discover more of the wonderful attributes of this legendary cat who has been the muse and inspiration for various works of art and learn more about its unique traits that have endeared it to many throughout the passing of history.

Glossary of Cat Terms

Abundism – Referring to a cat that has markings more prolific than is normal.

Acariasis – A type of mite infection.

ACF – Australian Cat Federation

Affix – A cattery name that follows the cat's registered name; cattery owner, not the breeder of the cat.

Agouti – A type of natural coloring pattern in which individual hairs have bands of light and dark coloring.

Ailurophile – A person who loves cats.

Albino – A type of genetic mutation which results in little to no pigmentation, in the eyes, skin, and coat.

Allbreed – Referring to a show that accepts all breeds or a judge who is qualified to judge all breeds.

Alley Cat – A non-pedigreed cat.

Alter – A desexed cat; a male cat that has been neutered or a female that has been spayed.

Amino Acid – The building blocks of protein; there are 22 types for cats, 11 of which can be synthesized and 11 which must come from the diet (see essential amino acid).

Anestrus – The period between estrus cycles in a female cat.

Any Other Variety (AOV) – A registered cat that doesn't conform to the breed standard.

ASH – American Shorthair, a breed of cat.

Back Cross – A type of breeding in which the offspring is mated back to the parent.

Balance – Referring to the cat's structure; proportional in accordance with the breed standard.

Barring – Describing the tabby's striped markings.

Base Color – The color of the coat.

Bicolor – A cat with patched color and white.

Blaze – A white coloring on the face, usually in the shape of an inverted V.

Bloodline – The pedigree of the cat.

Brindle – A type of coloring, a brownish or tawny coat with streaks of another color.

Castration – The surgical removal of a male cat's testicles.

Cat Show – An event where cats are shown and judged.

Cattery – A registered cat breeder; also, a place where cats may be boarded.

CFA – The Cat Fanciers Association.

Cobby – A compact body type.

Colony – A group of cats living wild outside.

Color Point – A type of coat pattern that is controlled by color point alleles; pigmentation on the tail, legs, face, and ears with an ivory or white coat.

Colostrum – The first milk produced by a lactating female; contains vital nutrients and antibodies.

Conformation – The degree to which a pedigreed cat adheres to the breed standard.

Cross Breed – The offspring produced by mating two distinct breeds.

Dam – The female parent.

Declawing – The surgical removal of the cat's claw and first toe joint.

Developed Breed – A breed that was developed through selective breeding and crossing with established breeds.

Down Hairs – The short, fine hairs closest to the body which keep the cat warm.

DSH – Domestic Shorthair.

Estrus – The reproductive cycle in female cats during which she becomes fertile and receptive to mating.

Fading Kitten Syndrome – Kittens that die within the first two weeks after birth; the cause is generally unknown.

Feral – A wild, untamed cat of domestic descent.

Gestation – Pregnancy; the period during which the fetuses develop in the female's uterus.

Guard Hairs – Coarse, outer hairs on the coat.

Harlequin – A type of coloring in which there are van markings of any color with the addition of small patches of the same color on the legs and body.

Inbreeding – The breeding of related cats within a closed group or breed.

Kibble – Another name for dry cat food.

Lilac – A type of coat color that is pale pinkish-gray.

Line – The pedigree of ancestors; family tree.

Litter – The name given to a group of kittens born at the same time from a single female.

Mask – A type of coloring seen on the face in some breeds.

Matts – Knots or tangles in the cat's fur.

Mittens – White markings on the feet of a cat.

Moggie – Another name for a mixed breed cat.

Mutation – A change in the DNA of a cell.

Muzzle – The nose and jaws of an animal.

Natural Breed – A breed that developed without selective breeding or the assistance of humans.

Neutering – Desexing a male cat.

Open Show – A show in which spectators are allowed to view the judging.

Pads – The thick skin on the bottom of the feet.

Particolor – A type of coloration in which there are markings of two or more distinct colors.

Patched – A type of coloration in which there is any solid color, tabby, or tortoiseshell color plus white.

Pedigree – A purebred cat; the cat's papers showing its family history.

Pet Quality – A cat that is not deemed of high enough standard to be shown or bred.

Piebald – A cat with white patches of fur.

Points – Also color points; markings of contrasting color on the face, ears, legs, and tail.

Pricked – Referring to ears that sit upright.

Purebred – A pedigreed cat.

Queen – An intact female cat.

Roman Nose – A type of nose shape with a bump or arch.

Scruff – The loose skin on the back of a cat's neck.

Selective Breeding – A method of modifying or improving a breed by choosing cats with desirable traits.

Senior – A cat that is more than 5 but less than 7 years old.

Sire – The male parent of a cat.

Solid – Also self; a cat with a single coat color.

Spay – Desexing a female cat.

Stud – An intact male cat.

Tabby – A type of coat pattern consisting of a contrasting color over a ground color.

Tom Cat – An intact male cat.

Tortoiseshell – A type of coat pattern consisting of a mosaic of red or cream and another base color.

Tri-Color – A type of coat pattern consisting of three distinct colors in the coat.

Tuxedo – A black and white cat.

Unaltered – A cat that has not been desexed.

Chapter Two: Russian Blue Cat in Focus

Russian Blue cats may often times look like your loving grandparents, your curious neighbor, your energetic pal, or that very playful sibling you always wanted. In whatever attitude or mood it appeals, you can expect it to make you appreciate life and make every moment count like you've never seen it before.

The Russian Blue is a unique and wonderful breed of cat but it may not be the right choice for everyone. Before you decide whether or not it might be the right pet for you and your family, you need to learn and invest a significant amount of time in getting to know these animals.

In this chapter you will receive an introduction to the Russian Blue cat breed including some basic facts and information as well as the history of how it came about.

This information, in combination with the practical information about keeping Russian Blue cats in the next chapter, will help you decide if this is the perfect cat companion for you.

Facts about the Russian Blue Cat

This outstandingly unique breed of a feline is a plush, shimmering pale hue of blue-gray, and its head bejeweled with a pair of bewitching emerald green eyes. Guard hairs are recognizably silver-tipped which gives the feline a silvery sheen and a lustrous appearance, completing the overall and very distinct look of the Russian Blue.

Historically, felines of all breeds have been utilized in the propagation, population, repopulation, development and improvement of other feline breeds. This fact holds true for our devoted Russian Blue as they too have been used to produce other breeds such as the Havana Brown. The Nebelung cat has the Russian Blue to thank for its contribution to the development of its kind.

They are presently utilized in Italy to help create Oriental Shorthairs that are healthier and more robust, calling this breed RUS4OSH in FIFe.

It may have been the brilliant green eyes of the Russian Blue Cat, which calls for immediate attention when laid sights upon, or the silvery blue-grey coat, shimmering with its every movement, which made it an eye-catching choice from amongst other felines. It would be safe to suppose that the absence of genetic issues in the Russian Blue, its lesser likelihood of inheriting troubling medical conditions, its vigorous physique and its mild temperament, would've been some of the criteria it possess that made it the likely selection for the job.

A Summary of Facts about the Russian Blue cat

The more you learn about your pet choice, the greater your advantage at gaining a good head start in preparing yourself, other caregivers and your home to welcoming your Russian Blue into your fold.

- Russian Blue cats have a noticeable, slightly upturned mouth giving it the appearance of giving a subtle smile similar to that of the Mona Lisa.

- According to folklore of the past, Russian Blues were a fixture in the rooms of newborns to ward off and chase away evil and malevolent spirits.

- A Russian Blue cat is featured as a trained assassin in the Warner Bros hit movie Cats & Dogs.

- A diluted gene is the reason why Russian Blues are blue. This gene which is responsible for the blue-gray coloring of the feline is actually a diluted form of the black-hair gene.
- Nyan Cat, the half-cat, half-pop tart Internet sensation and animated meme is based on Marty, the illustrators very own Rusian Blue.

- Many Tom and Jerry fans speculate that Tom, with his blue-gray hue and bright green eyes, is a Russian Blue.

- There are some Russian Blues who are born with "ghost stripes" which are in fact, faint tabby markings which disappear when the kitten matures.

The Russian Blue Cat History

Much has been speculated about the origins of the Russian Blue Cat, but determination of its actual beginnings is vague. However it is strongly believed and suggested that these mysterious looking felines originated from the port of Arkhangelsk, Russia.

They are sometimes also given the moniker Archangel Blues. It is surmised that seafarers took a liking to the Russian Blue and brought them along from the shores of the Archangel Isles to the ports of Great Britain and other parts of Northern Europe in the 1860's.

The first ever recorded sighting and grand appearance of the Russian Blue was documented to have taken place in 1875 in England, at the Crystal Palace, when it was given the name Archangel Cat.

The electrifyingly attractive Russian Blue competed in a class which included all other felines of the blue color until 1912, which was when it was given a category and class all on its own.

The Russian Blue breed, after WWII, was mainly developed in Scandinavia and England. Shortly after the war, a noticeable lack of numbers in the population of the Russian Blue gave way for cross breeding with the Siamese

Cat. That's why there is somewhat a resemblance in the breed.

Russian Blues were in the United States of America before the said war. However it was not until the post-war era that American breeders came up with a method to create the modern day Russian Blue which is most sought after and seen in the United States today.

This method was accomplished by mixing the bloodlines of both the British Russian and Scandinavian Russian Blue cats. The traits of the Siamese have presently been pretty much bred out the slate-gray/blue color and short hair style is regularly seen in cats of mixed-breed which can affect showers and breeders because of mislabeling a feline as a Russian Blue.

Types of Russian Blue Cats

Stories of the origins of the Russian Blue cat remain vague and blurry. Legends abound, stories have been told, and lore passed on from one generation to the next.

The elusive truth of the actual beginnings of the Russian Blue cat only adds to its mystique and fans the fire of curiosity. The elegantly, long and slender physique of this devotedly loyal feline, has been catching eyes and hearts for as long as it silently entered the social scene and shared stomping ground with us two-legged folk.

Appearing to be larger than it actually is, the Russian Blue owes this illusion of grandness to its thick, dense, silver-blue coat, is believed to have developed to adaptively insulate this beautiful creature from the harsh winters in the cold regions of Russia.

This vagueness of its origins reflects in the many names the Russian Blue went by; Archangels Blue, Maltese Blue, Foreign Blue and Spanish Blue are just some of the older names it was called. Despite these strong evidence points the breed to have originated from Northern Europe.

People from as early as the 16th century has sighted the Russian Blue cat; there were also pictures found that appeared to be the Russian Blue on the Kola Peninsula in countries like Denmark and Norway as well as in the Central and Northern parts of Sweden and Russia. Belief of the felines being in Russia the longest is given proof in the folkloric photos English seafarers took with them from the shores and harbors of Russia, these pictures which hung originally in the cabins and chalets of the Russian locals.

Some of these curious photos show pictures of blue cats being buried by dozens upon dozens of mice. Curious indeed! These were the same sailors who not only brought back pictures of this blue cat but in fact, adopted and brought home the blue cat itself. They had purchased these blue cats in the harbor town of Anchangelsk, kept them onboard -the cats earned their keep by hunting mice and rodents on the ship - and later, upon arrival on the shores of England, the cats were sold to the locals at markets flanking the harbor of the slate rock of England.

The blue cat from off the ships of English seafarers were lauded to be excellent hunters of mice and this was proven true by stories of the men on the ships who witnessed their hunting prowess and efficiency as unofficial onboard rodent patrol. The cat's luxuriously thick and gleaming fur mimicking beaver fur was a winning quality which made it an extremely popular house pet. The early English Chronicles mentions the Russian Blue as early as 1860.

It could have be possible that the feline enjoyed recognition from as early as 1553, which would've been around the era when English merchants found, in Anchangelsk their trade colony consisting mostly of timber and animal skins - which for they purposed the isles - to export back to their home England.

Some of the more legendary tales of the Russian Blue has it playing a royal part in the courts of the palace of Tsar Nicholas the Second, who was said to take in a Russian Blue into his kingdom. Tales of the feline possessing magical powers that would protect households to ward off evil spirits proliferated. This was the reason why these cats were often placed within the chambers of a newborn or even placed in the cribs themselves beside the new barn.

In another royal tale, it has been told and retold that Catherine the Great gifted a blue cat to the British Royal Family. Whether these stories are true or not has not been given concrete evidence but one thing is certain. The Russian blue cats from the land of Archangelsk have been frequently brought to the isles of England from the second half of the 19th century.

It was in the 1870 when the first breeders showed interest in this blue cat. The breeders made the decision to use the blue felines from Angelsk to upgrade the domesticated British Blue.

The fur of the British Blue cat was not as lush or as good as the Archangelsk cats silvery fur. Inclination to theses blue cats resulted in the showing of the first blue felines from Russia in 1880. And as a result, interest toward this blue cat soared and from 1883 onward, blue cats imported from Russia increased exponentially.

English, Scandinavian and American Type Russian Blues

It is safe to say that the English bred Russian Blue feline stands at the advent of all Russian. In spite of this, due to different breeding programs and methods across the globe, the Russian Blue has evolved to three variants.

English Type

The English type Russian Blue is known to be somewhat heavier. Their coats are good and plush and are considered to be middle blue. The whisker pads are much more pronounced giving the face a larger look. Their eyes look heavy-lidded like they've just had a few drinks. They are quite reserved and quiet.

Scandinavian Type

This Scandinavian Russian Blue shares many characteristics with the English type Russian. They do look a tad bit different in the ear location and their coats are a bit on the darker shade and are less soft to the feel than that of the English type. Their body structure is more rounded in shape compared to the absolute almond shape eyes of the English Russian.

American Type

The American type is the Russian Blue which is farthest in the original looks of the Russian Blue. The American Russian is longer, but smaller than the English type felines. The coat of the American Russians is also different from the two previously mentioned Russian types; theirs is lighter. There has been a clamor for cats with lighter fur with green eyes. Their eyes are rounder than the two other types. Their ears are much wider apart on top of their heads. The whisker pads are less pronounced but the notable Mona Lisa smile is still ever present, nonetheless, on this beautiful feline.

Chapter Three: Russian Blue Cat Requirements

The Russian Blue Cat is a feline known to be quite healthy in comparison to other pedigreed feline breeds and would need very little from you in terms of its grooming care. In the following passages, you will find out about the needs and requirements of the Russian Blue. This chapter aims to show what is expected from you as caregiver of this magnificent creature. It also aims to show you the pros and cons of keeping a RB cat as a family pet.

You will also learn if keeping more than one is a possibility. Here you will read about the cost and ease of caring for a Russian Blue. This chapter also includes a rundown of the initial costs you will be looking at upon acquisition of a Russian Blue as well as the monthly costs of caring for one.

Licensing and Registration

In New South Wales, all canines and felines, with the exception of some exempt dogs and cats, is to be registered by the 6th month of its existence. The registration cost is a one-time payment which covers the pet (dog or cat) for its lifetime, notwithstanding changes in ownership. It is encouraged that the canine or feline be identified in terms of gender before it is registered. This requirement is a staple in most Australian and New Zealand states. Information on cat registry requirements for CFA in the United States can be found in Chapter Eight of this book.

Should You Opt for More Than One Russian Blue cat?

The countless reasons of attraction to this breed do not stop with its obviously stunning physical appearance, nor does it end with the mysterious smile that it seems to perpetually sport. The Russian Blue cat, with its playful disposition and remarkable intelligence, has been a consistently, well sought after pet favorite, reportedly said to be a perfect furry companion and household addition for many families.

Families with older children and existing feline-friendly pets have been said to welcome the Russian Blue with hardly any hiccups because of its even-temperedness. Families with older children of 10-years and up enjoy daily family routines which involve and include the growing feline. The blue-streak fur ball will certainly be an additional source of happiness and inspiration when brought into a family.

This is because the silver-blue, roundish feline gets along famously well with people. Just give it time. And space. And it'll soon enough warm up to you.

It is a gentle cat who can seem somewhat shy when surrounded by strangers. But shy is hardly what this fellow is. True to its blue-blooded nature, the Russian Blue prefers to reserve making conclusions of anyone or anything until it has observed, studied, surveyed and gotten to know everything and everyone. Once it makes up its mind, it has no qualms expressing how valuable you are. They are openly affectionate and deeply devoted to their loved ones and guardians.

Their keen sensitivity toward their caregiver's mood has been noted time and again and its sensitivity to its humans is known to be one of the many positive traits of the Russian Blue Cat. It will feel the shift in its guardian's emotions, almost mirroring the inner workings of its caregiver. It will get nearer to you and offer you comfort in times of distress or worry.

The Russian Blue is a sweet home companion who will be glad to greet you upon your arrival at the door. It will be happy to find a spot next to you and just be in the general area where you are and where it can share space with and be close to you.

Observation of these felines, since humans started taking them in, has revealed that they favor and enjoy a game of "fetch". Identify a favorite toy of it which it can carry between its small jaws, show it to your RBC, toss it at a decent distance and watch your RBC eagerly fetch the object. In fact, if you aren't the sort to toss around a ball, you may soon be taught by our patient little friend on how to throw one. Russian Blues have been noted to sometimes dominate caregivers who indulge them. So, if you are the alpha-type, you would want to set rules and boundaries at the onset of the relationship.

Being of a relatively calm and tranquil sort, your RB will find a quieter and safer space when there is a lot of commotion and activity in the home. The RB will retreat away from chaotic noise such as when you pull out the vacuum cleaner or when you use any kitchen machinery which emits grinding, chopping or whirring sounds.

It is reserved and would rather keep to itself in social situations which it may find too overwhelming to partake in. It doesn't warm up to strangers easily, which works well for Russian Blue guardians because this trait of seeming aloofness and suspiciousness keeps would-be cat-nappers away.

Once socialized into a family, given time to allow it to settle down and survey its new surroundings, the elegant Russian Blue will be open and welcoming to get to know you and the rest of the family. It will shadow your movements around the house and try to help you out in your daily doings and may even chime in its two-cents worth should it find your labor to be a little lackluster. When spoken to, it will talk back but it is generally a quiet cat, happy to just be around you.

Russian Blues are rambunctious playmates and can get pretty excited during playtime. There is nothing more heartwarming and amusing to the eyes than seeing a bunch of happy, smiling Russian Blue fur-balls, rolling and frolicking around your living room to complete your day. It is no wonder that many cat aficionados and guardians can't help talking about their furry wards when they are away from them. When something good happens to someone, people tend to share it to anyone they know because they're unable to hold back the joy seeping from them and needing to infect others with it. This is how a cat-owner would describe the close bond they developed and share with their four-legged, blue-grey streak of a fur ball.

Once it integrates into your home and family, the Russian Blue will be glad to spend time with anyone in the family who pays it careful and gentle mind. This level of trust is reserved only toward people it holds dear and is in often contact with. Hesitation t will openly show and display its trust, affection and devotion with no hesitation or reservations.

Many felines, whose other motto could be "Stranger danger", must be one of the mottos of the Russian Blue as well who would most likely keep a good space between itself and a stranger. It will be comfortable to study a stranger from a safe, distance but will not risk a stressful situation and get closer. Friends of the family will later be introduced to your Russian Blue so they will eventually get used to unhurried social activities as time goes by.

Except perhaps for mealtimes, when it can be quite vocal and excited, the Russian Blue cat is relatively soft-spoken and quiet-voiced. However, chat it up and it will talk to you as well. It has a penchant for using its voice and its vocabulary when you converse with it and it will be happy to lounge and catch up with you about the day's events.

The Russian Blue loves when it is shown attention and affection by its guardians; it appreciates gentle pats and tender, loving strokes on its head. It loves to perch on a window and enjoy the sights and sounds of the world outside. Of course, it is most content in the comfort and security you give it inside your home.

They are rare and highly sought after, so it is strongly recommended that you keep your Russian Blue as an indoor pet with limited, supervised forays outside of the home attended by you or another caregiver.

Russian Blue Cats Behavior with Humans and Pets

Russian Blue Cats are even-tempered and very amiable toward the family to which it belongs. It gravitates toward members of the family who revere it with respect and extend kindness toward it.

Information on the proper handling of a Russian Blue is to be communicated and cascaded to everyone in the family so that they are aware of how to properly treat the sensitive Russian Blue. It will tolerate and put up with the handling of clumsy toddlers and it would seem as if it recognizes that there is no harm meant. They may tend to walk away or stay out of reach of people who may handle them a little clumsily. So be making sure of your presence when the cat is around young toddlers is of vital importance at the onset of indoctrination.

With that said it is imperative that potential caregivers know how to handle a RB with gentle care so that it gains confidence in its surroundings and develops trust toward the humans it lives with at home. Russian Blues are to be protected from rough handling and treatment, so it is necessary to supervise very young children when they are present with the feline.

The Russian Blue is open and accepting of other pets, including cat-friendly canines, so long as they are not menaced, chased or harassed by them. It is strongly advised that introduction of pets be done in a slow and controlled environment, ideally with another caregiver present, to ensure they are given time to get used to each other. You need to also give them enough time, room and space to learn to get along.

The Russian Blue is a good pet choice for people who have never owned cats. A small investment of time and patience will be sufficient to successfully incorporate the feline into the home dynamics.

What does it Cost to take in a Russian Blue cat?

The Russian Blue Cat is one of the easiest feline breed to care for and share a home with.

The Russian Blue cat is a quiet cat and likes its surroundings to be fuss-free and non-chaotic. It languishes in tranquil calm. It will teach you a few things about enjoying each moment as it comes as well as appreciating, and living in, the present - which are good life lessons we can gain from and learn given the fast-paced life most of us live today.

Initial Costs

You will have to get your finances ready and sorted out before deciding to buy a Russian Blue. Here you will find out everything you need to know about what to expect when acquiring a RB cat.

Price of a Russian Blue Kitten

First of all, the important bit of information you need to know now is the average price of a Russian Blue kitten. Knowing the average price allows you to evaluate the good offers from the bad ones.

The average market price of a pet quality Russian Blue ranges anywhere from $400-$600.

Champion lines for breeding and showing are even more costly, with prices ranging anywhere from $800 - $3000 for each kitten.

Shipping Costs

Shipping fees are to be factored into the initial costs as this will be a considerable amount depending on how far away you live from the breeder. Since Russian Blues are quite rare, it may be possible that you shall have to order your Russian Blue kitten outside of your home state or country. Shipping costs may vary from $175-$350.

To determine this, you want to get in touch with shipping and handling company to ask about its shipping prices for pets. Shipping and handling fees will also be depend on the location of origin.

Cat Supplies

Some Russian Blue breeders will give you little extras like toys and other things your Russian Blue used whilst under their care. However, if your Russian Blue is coming in from a faraway place, these things will have to be counted into the shipping costs.

Here are other things you will need to prepare for initially before you welcome your Russian Blue to your home;

- Kitten Food: $15-$30
- Treats: $5 - $15
- Bed and blankets: $25 - $75
- Feeders and bowls: You want to invest in the more sturdy kind which are easy to clean and are non-toxic - $50 - $150
- Collar, Harness and/or Leash: $5 - $20
- Brush: $4 - $50
- Trimmers and Clippers: $6 - $50
- Litter: $5 - $35
- Litter Boxes: $15 - $200
- Waste Disposal: $3 - $30
- Filters and deodorants: $4 - $25
- Liners and mats: $2 - $40
- Toys: $1 - $50
- Toy Crate: $10 - $150
- Cat carrier: $25 - $200
- Vaccination for kittens: $50 - $100
- Vet visit: $35 - $50

These prices will fluctuate greatly depending on your taste. It is strongly recommended that you invest well on the things your Russian Blue will be using for the long haul like its bed, feeding bowls (recommended is the slow-feeding bowl to dissuade the cat from eating too fast or too much), brush, and of course, do not to scrimp on the quality of food you give it as this will greatly influence the health of the cat both physically and mentally.

Monthly Costs

The monthly cost of taking care of your Russian Blue will be more stable in terms of consistency as time passes. You will not need to spend as much as you did initially since you would have invested in the more expensive sundries before your Russian Blue comes home.

You won't to be stuck with footing the bills for expenses your income cannot afford. So, it is just wise to get your finances sorted out for the monthly cost you will incur once your Russian Blue is home.

Here is a quick look at what you should expect to spend each month.

- Kitten Food: $15-$30
- Treats: $5 - $15
- Litter: $5 - $35
- Waste Disposal: $3 - $30
- Filters and deodorants: $4 - $25
- Liners and mats: $2 - $40

Pros and Cons of Owning a Russian Blue cat

The Russian Blue Cat is widely known to be one of the healthiest of felines amongst most, if not all, cat breeds. The reason for it enjoying robust, sound health is due to the fact that the feline is a naturally occurring breed.

Russian Blues are not prone to illnesses like most other felines, which make caring for one (or more) a lot easier than if caring for another feline breed. This exquisite feline has enjoyed the company of people for as long as humans began welcoming and taking in four-legged beasts into their homes.

As a rule of thumb, no matter which pet you decide to take in, research you do prior to acquisition allows you to set reasonable expectations for the day when you actually drive home with your own little buddy. This time of learning is crucial to the success of your upcoming new pairing, the smooth transition of incorporating the new addition to you home, life and family as well as your desire to take in these furry loving creatures as companions and pets.

You will have to do a lot of calling, asking questions and studying to empower yourself to know all you need to know about the background, history, breeding methods and possible medical conditions an animal may be averse to and prone. Whenever taking in a new pet it is but wise and sound to discuss possible illnesses your pet may contract with a pet health care provider - namely, your vet. You, as its caregiver, will have to study up on what to avoid keeping your cat safe and healthy.

The Russian Blue may occasionally suffer from stress and its caregiver must be in the position to recognize the symptoms when a Russian Blue experiences a bout of stress and what you can do to intervene. Stress and anxiety are manifestations of fear and insecurity in the cat.

It is pretty independent and will have no problems keeping itself occupied when you are at work, but other than food, it thrives to be the best in your presence and companionship. Neglecting to set aside time for it when you get back home - if it happens often enough - may result in it developing anxiety. Be sure to make time every day to visit with your RB so that it doesn't feel neglected or ignored.

A trusted and experienced vet will be able to give you the low down on the basic diet that your feline pet requires. Be mindful to give it proper feeding portions and avoid over-feeding your Russian Blue to prevent it from gaining unwanted weight. Over-feeding any pet increases the likelihood of obesity which in turn causes other health related problems.

This feline is a playful breed with a notably high level of intelligence. It is not the sort of feline who will go into overdrive when it gets too excited, so you will not have to deal with an overly hyperactive cat should you decide to bring home a Russian Blue. But it does know how to have fun and is a great playmate. It will not be unusual to see the normally reserved RB let loose once in a while and put down its guards.

Chapter Four: Acquiring Your Very Own Russian Blue Cat

You've come this far and have read up more on what it would take for you to adopt, take in or acquire a Russian Blue cat. It is now time for you to find out how to research procedures, seek out reputable breeders and to find out about humane methods of Russian Blue production which will ensure the future well-being and health of your Russian Blue cat.

This chapter aims to assist you in finding out who to talk to and where to acquire your very own Russian Blue cat. Whether you choose to adopt or purchase one, here you will find information vital to the success and health of your would-be Russian Blue companion.

Where Should You Look to Acquire a Russian Blue Cat?

Many upstanding, reputable breeders maintain websites. It can be quite challenging to sift out the good ones from the bad. You will have to watch out for and be aware of red flags that will indicate the honesty - or lack thereof - of a breeder. Some red flags to watch out for is the constant availability of kittens, giving a future guardian any choice of kitten, allowing the accessibility to make payments online via your credit card, as well as the presence of multiple litters in their facilities.

These may sound convenient and standard procedure, but beware, because reputable breeders are nearly never associated with these situations or options. Reputable breeders like to deal with potential guardians personally. They want to share information and find out what a potential guardian has done in preparation of a likely pet addition.

Reputable breeders will also not readily have kittens available. Breeders of good repute will put you on a waiting list most of the time as there is a relatively small number of breeders who work with this breed.

There is no sure-fire guarantee that the information here will help you better identify the intentions of a breeder. Nor does it assure you of the good or ill repute of the breeder you will choose to deal with, so asking the right questions are equally important when seeking out an honest and ethical breeder.

Some good questions you will want to ask any breeder you talk to is what sort of guarantee they give to kittens under their care. You will also want to ask what they would do if the kitten is later found to have a serious health condition. You will also want to discuss how the kitten was socialized; you will want to witness how the kittens interact and respond to the breeder. This will give you an idea of their personality and will assist in determining the amount of handling the litter of kittens has received.

Set expectations and be ready to wait for at least 6 months (sometimes more) for the right kitten to be made available. Since Russian Blues are a rare breed, Russian Blue breeders may not be easy to find even if they are near your vicinity. Use this time to do further research as you prepare and outfit your home for the eventual addition to your home.

Breeders of good standing will not release kittens to new homes until they are ready to be separated from its mother, or when it has weaned off the teat. This will mean you will have to wait another 12-16 weeks after their birth to have them join you. This time can be put to good use for you to make certain you have covered all bases and your home and its surroundings is ready for the new member to join the family ranks.

Qualities of a Reputable Breeder

Primarily, you will want to make certain that you only deal with an upstanding breeder as this will minimize the problems of taking in a sick kitten. Being in the know and ready for all eventualities is not only smart, it is an imperative.

The following are tips on seeking out an honest Russian Blue cat breeder:

- Collect and gather as much information as you possibly can about the breeders in your area. Get referrals from other Russian Blue cat guardians who are experienced and who may already have a database of reputable breeders. Network with and keep in contact with experienced Russian Blue guardians, groomers, pet shops and veterinary clinics - they can be good sources of information as to where you can find a healthy Russian Blue cat.

- Scrutinize and research breeders who have websites. Look up their reputation, ranking and license. Save yourself from frustration, stress and worry and only deal with breeders with a high success rate.

- Don't be taken for a ride. Ask questions and lots of them. Asking questions about breeding methods, procedures and practices ensures that you will be ready for any and all eventualities the Russian Blue may or may not encounter in the future.

- Ask about the breeder's program and what methods they employ during the mating period. Don't be afraid to ask for assurances - you need to be aware of what measures the breeder takes to largely eliminate or at the very least prevent the transmission of congenital conditions that can be passed on to young Russian Blue kittens.

- Immediately turn away from breeders on your list who give flowery, shady, dodgy and seemingly uninformed responses. Make certain that you deal only with breeders who have a good success rate and have been reputed to be humane in dealing with the breeding process.

- Do not think twice about eliminating breeders on your list who refuse to answer questions you may ask about the cats' history, health, method of breeding and anything else related to the future welfare and overall well-being of the feline.

- Hop into your car and take a road trip. Ask to visit the breeder's facilities. A breeder who has nothing to hide will welcome you immediately and will gladly give you a tour around their facilities. You want to look at the facilities with your own eyes and check out if the shelter is kept sanitary. Willingness and transparency to attend to and respond to queries from possible Russian Blue caregivers is a positive attribute and these breeders should be marked for strong consideration.

- Upstanding breeders will also be asking their own set of questions. These breeders are not just out to make a quick buck. They are equally concerned about the future wellbeing of the feline and will ask questions that will determine if you are indeed a suitable caregiver of this precious life.

- If you decide on purchasing a Russian Blue kitten, you will have to place a deposit to get the ball rolling. Do not forget to ask about the breeders terms as finances will be discussed. Once you and the breeder come to an agreement, you can mark off one of the first tasks on your list as done. Make sure that you are furnished with papers that would reflect your initial payment and that all sundries are itemized.

Adopt a Russian Blue cat from a Rescue

Adopting from a shelter is one sure fire way of dissuading the operations of shady, fly-by-night breeders. It also garners you points for a good deed done when you opt to rescue a Russian Blue from a bleak future. This avenue to acquiring a Russian Blue entails very little in terms of initial investment and the returns are far greater than you would ever imagine. The insurmountable benefits of adopting a Russian Blue cat is limitless and if you are lucky enough you might just find one ready and waiting for your loving care at a nearby shelter.

The obvious and distinct difference of getting a Russian Blue cat from a reputable breeder to rescuing one from an uncertain future at a pet shelter is with the latter you would have given the poor feline a chance at living a better life and being in a home that it deserves.

A rescue Russian Blue may also have the advantage of being house trained and housebroken which allows you more quality time into getting to know the cat as well as getting it integrated with yourself and your family, getting them blended into your daily routine will almost be like taking a walk in the park.

List of Websites of Breeders and Rescue Adoption

Russian Blue Cat Breeders

TICA
<http://www.tica.org/find-a-breeder/item/304-russian-blue-breeders>

Gumtree
<https://www.gumtree.com/cats/uk/russian+blue>

Pet Overstock

<https://pets.overstock.com/pets/Cat,Russian-Blue,/species,breed,/?distance=25>

Pets4Homes UK

<https://www.pets4homes.co.uk/sale/cats/russian-blue/>

Dariushka
<http://www.dariushka.com/>

Bluebebop
<http://bluebebop.webs.com/>

Adopt-a-Pet
<http://www.adoptapet.com/s/russian-cats-for-adoption>

Russian Cats
<http://www.russiancats.com/>

Selecting a Healthy Russian Blue cat

These robust cats are known to be one of the healthiest felines in the spectrum. Enjoying an average life expectancy of 10-15 years, with some noted to have lived for as long as 25 years, it is one feline who leads quite a healthy life because of their resilience and fortunate circumstance.

This stroke of good genes is due to the fact that they are a naturally occurring breed, decreasing, or totally eliminating, the likelihood of genetic abnormalities that often plague other feline breeds.

You will want to deal with breeders who screen and test their cats before they release them to future guardians. Those who are upstanding in their field would have also had initial inoculation done before the cat is handed over to your eager arms.

How to Feline-Proof Your Home

The following information aims to help you to start preparing and fitting your home to welcome your new Russian Blue cat:

- Keep food out of sight and reach. Store them in cupboards or stack them in a closed pantry away from your buddy. Make sure that any food that is set outside the fridge or pantry is sealed in tightly covered spill-proof containers. Clapping and calling out the name of your Russian Blue usually does the job of dissuading it from further mischief and curiosity.

- Felines have a natural tendency to hunt, rummage and scrounge for food and curiosities. Stave off this innate habit of theirs by making certain your trash bins are tightly covered and won't spill out in the event of cat curiosity.

- Cats are naturally curious and will usually play with small objects that they can push around and play with. Store away tiny valuables if you suspect your little fur ball is the sort of cat who likes to play with small, shiny objects. You will have to make sure that there are no loose strings or hanging ropes they could get tangled in, so keeping wires folded or protected from unwanted gnawing is a measure you would want to take to somehow guarantee its safety.

- Vitamins, medication, and/or prescription drugs are to be kept away from its reach and hidden from sight. The dangers of having your feline ingest a meant-for-human pill is the last thing you want to happen and will warrant a trip to the emergency room. The discomfort the cat has to endure to expel this from its body can be uncomfortable. Best that caregivers avoid this preventable trip to vet by keeping all medicine locked away.

- Cleaning supplies you use around the home usually contain highly toxic chemicals which can poison and cause great harm your new friend. Do store them away where your Russian Blue kitten can't see or find these products which will certainly cause them great harm.

- Should your feline be allowed to wander around the house and its perimeter make certain that you do not neglect to cat-proof your garage too. Cats are known to prefer perching on high places. Make sure that there is no heavy equipment or tools which they may push over the edge which may hurt them or people in the home.

- This bit is very important for those who have house plants or foliage growing around their home; there are many, countless plants that pose danger to felines. Determine that the greenery surrounding your home is non - toxic to your Russian Blue cat. In the event that you determine that there are plants in or around your homes which are toxic to your feline, consider replanting them away from the area where your cat is allowed to roam. You may also opt to barricade these plants or altogether replace them with plants that are non - toxic to cats. Poisoning from plants which are toxic or harmful when ingested by cats is a very real concern and should be high on your list of things to avoid.

- Keep in mind that cats have a tendency to get carried away when they are at play. Dealing with more than one pet can also be quite a handful. To avoid the possibility of electrocution when your feline is in a curious mood or when rough housing with their furry pals, use plastic covers to plug unused electrical sockets.

- It is not a surprise that some cats have an aversion to gnawing at strings, ropes and electric wires that mimic string. Feline-proof exposed wires with those nifty wire covers that will discourage them from chewing on a live wire which their teeth may damage and cause them electrocution.

There are a lot more tips than what is listed here to keep your Russian Blue cat safe within your home. These preventive and safety tips will not only benefit your friendly feline, it will also serve you and your family well so that you can keep your home intact and safe from accidents. Remove things that can be harmful to your feline and any minimize the possible incidence of danger posed to your family members.

Chapter Five: Maintenance for Your Russian Blue Cats

Keeping and maintaining a space where your Russian Blue can confidently roam will be one of the things you will need to prepare for at great lengths. Doing so will almost guarantee a fuss-free transition.

In this chapter you will learn how to take care of your Russian blue and you'll also be given additional information regarding the equipment you need to use to make sure they become healthy.

Tips on How to Cat-Proof Your Home to Keep Your Cat Happy Indoors and Outdoors

Felines are known to be relentlessly curious beings. The abundance of sayings and quotes referencing the mischief and precarious situations cats can find them in is enough to support this claim. Russian Blues, with their calm characteristic and tendency to find tranquil in chaos will still need to be protected from things which may pose or cause them harm because they too can be rough players during downtime playtime.

Cat-proofing your home will not only benefit your new RB feline and guarantee it a space which is safe, feline-friendly and cat-worthy, it will also give you the peace of mind that you and your family will co-exist safely with your new Russian Blue, harmoniously.

Take note of the important things to keep in mind whilst you make plans to cat-proof your home and areas around your house where your cat is allowed to wander.

Poisonous plants: felines have an innate aversion to munch on grass and foliage. Be aware that most plants are toxic to felines and even non-poisonous plants can be reason for diarrhea and vomiting in cats. Determine what plants flank your home. Should there be toxic plants around your home, you may want to consider barricading, replanting them farther away, or completely replacing them with plants that are good for cats.

Russian Blues are smart felines. Remember that they are highly trainable cats with very keen intelligence. Aside from their inclination to play "fetch", it has been noted that RBs learn actions by observation. Many RBs have acquired the skill of opening closed doors just by studying how its guardian does this. It is therefore strongly advised that guardians of this intelligent breed keep dangerously toxic cleaning supplies away from the sight, reach and scent of your cat. Use child-proof latches to keep your cat from eating, chewing on or licking these very harmful chemicals.

All human medicine poses great danger to any pet when ingested. Make sure that all medication, vitamins and supplements - whether over-the-counter or prescribed - are out of your feline's reach. Be sure that no pills are left lying out where it can be found and accidentally ingested.

Store your fragile valuables away from the general area where your cat is allowed to roam, play and live. Felines are great explorers who live on satisfying their curiosity. They will jump on and off furniture and may accidentally knock over breakable treasures you've carefully collected. Save your cat a tongue-lashing and store these

valuable objects where they are not reached by your curious
Russian Blue.

You will want to unplug electrical cords that are not
in use - cats are great chewers and are easily attracted by
anything that imitates string. You won't want your cat to
suffer an electric shock when it chews on a live wire. You
may use those commercially manufactured wire covers to
protect wires from a curious cat. You will also want to cover
up any unused electrical sockets with plastic socket covers
lest your playful feline get its claw in places it shouldn't be.
These measures will keep your cat from getting a nasty
electric shock.

Anything that mimics string can be a hazard to your
friendly feline. Keep blind cords and drapery ropes coiled
and out of its reach. Your cat may manage to strangle
themself or get caught around a cord. Minimize the dangers
to your RB inside the house by taking stock of things it can
mistake for playthings.

Check all unlikely places where cats may hang out.
Felines are known to take a liking to staying in small, dark
and quiet spaces so you will want to check dryers, washers,
refrigerators, freezers, dresser drawers and most especially,
the under belly of cars for their presence. You want to call
out the felines name when checking. You can honk the horn
of your car to make sure your cat did not camp out and fall

asleep under one of the tires while you weren't looking. This is a good time to remind the potential guardian that the RB is best kept as an indoor cat to spare it from larger-animal attacks, would be cat-thieves, contracting disease and illness from other animals and vehicular accidents.

Table cloths which are set out act as invitation to investigative felines. Kittens will most likely try to climb the table cloth to inspect what's atop. This could lead to your best china shattering in a million tiny bits and an unexpected emergency trip to the vet.

Cover all toilets in the house with toilet lids. Keep these lids down when the toilet isn't in use as a curious kitten may fall into the bowl with no way of getting out on its own. This is especially important when you are at work or away from home.

Cats are deft climbers and they will most often find their way into the kitchen sink sooner than you would think. Learning to do things by witnessing, what to you are, inane actions can be amusing as much as it could be dangerous. Cover garbage disposal switches from their prying, curious paws lest they learn to work the garbage disposal switch and get into serious trouble.

Once more, you want to keep your Russian Blue indoors as an indoor cat - this measure of security will ward off would-be cat-nappers from carting your RB away. You will want to make sure that your door and window screens do not have tears from which they can exit. You will want to have securely fastened screens and sturdy latches to lessen the risk of your feline slipping out of the safety of its home unnoticed.

Toys and Accessories for Your Russian Blue

Your Russian Blue will spend most of its lifetime in the safety and comfort of your home. It is therefore wise to invest in entertainment that would engage it mentally as well as physically.

There are many available toys in the market that will keep your cat occupied and busy. Check out mechanical toys it can operate with simple levers. Look into getting your RB bells and chimes they can flick and tap. Engage them in mind puzzle games to continuously sharpen their innate talents.

A laser-light pointer which they can chase after and follow is one inexpensive toy that you can get practically anywhere. This can create extended periods of fun and active rudimentary exercise.

Teasers are also very effective entertainment tools that will keep your feline fit with cardio exercises which will give the cat reason to jump, chase and run after said toy. Soft, squeaky, spongy toys are great toys to wrestle with and spend energy on for times when it is home alone.

Socializing Your Cat

When in the midst of bustling surroundings it can be quite reserved and will most likely opt to survey its environment from a perch before it decides to join in or pass up the opportunity for socialization.

Because of their inherent intelligence they are easily trainable felines who can be taught to do tricks and have been observed to be great at the game "fetch". They are famous for figuring out how their guardians do everyday things like opening doors, throwing switches on, or opening covered containers, etc.

Unless brought up in an actively bustling household, the Russian Blue will usually be seen as detached when in the company of or when around strangers. They are generally considered as a reserved and quiet breed, given a few exceptions as no two cats, like every individual, share twin traits, personalities, or characteristics.

Russian Blues, like most felines of any breed, are fierce hunters of smaller creatures, such as birds, rabbits, small mammals, rodents and reptiles. These are innate skills and abilities many felines share and have been known to possess as means of sustenance and/or survival.

Chapter Six: Nutritional Needs of Russian Blue Cats

This section of the book is aimed at discussing the nutrition and food your Russian Blue cat will require. It will reveal what you should and should not feed your feline to successfully raise it. You will find out about foods that it requires for a healthy life and foods which are bad for them and that you should thereby avoid.

Like all things living, a feline's health hinges on the quality of food it eats. Make it your business to understand what your cat needs in order to stave off sickness. Your diligence in this matter of feeding and food will pay off in the long run and you will think yourself for thinking ahead.

The Nutritional Needs of Russian Blue Cats

As with people and other pets, RBC will thrive best and be at its healthiest with the proper nutrition. So choosing the proper foods that will meet its nutritional requirements is a must.

Remember that the RBC is one of the feline breeds least likely to be prone to feline illnesses, so you will be able to rest easier knowing that caring for it will not be as complicated.

Choosing the right foods to feed your new RB cat will be crucial to its continued good health. Today, feline guardians have a world of choices when choosing what sort of foods to feed their pets. Empower yourself and study up on what ingredients manufacturers use to produce their pet food. Learn to read labels and decipher complicated-sounding ingredients. Know the jargons and wordings manufacturers use to market their products.

Do your research and ask reputable breeders for recommendations they may be able to offer. Talk to your pet's health provider about your RBs diet and have the vet determine which kind of food will best work to your cat's advantage.

Feeding Your Russian Blue: From Kitten to Maturity

Food is on the top of a Russian Blues priority list, closely followed by its desire and need for your love and attention. The diet of a Russian Blue is not demanding nor does it require anything specific in its diet - in short they have no uncommon needs when it comes to nutrition. They are known to be hearty eaters and are not picky about the type of cat food given to them. They are usually satisfied with any sort of cat food and will demand a second helping.

They are masters at convincing you that you haven't fed them enough and will beg you for more. Do not give in. Your cat will try to get away with asking for more and if you give in to its chiding you would have encouraged a bad habit of overeating, which can lead to obesity and a life less active.

Overeating can cause obesity and cats suffering from this are prone to bone and joint problems due to the excess weight it has to carry. And this condition can be exorbitantly exaggerated by the cat not wanting to move, play, jump about or exercise.

The recommended frequency is three separate feedings throughout the day for a Russian Blue kitten until the kitten is 7 months old. Once past that 7 month milestone, reduce the frequency of feeding your Russian Blue to two times a day.

Experts and seasoned caregivers of the Russian Blue suggest feeding the cat a premium dry cat food which is preferably grain free. Grain free foods mean they have less "fillers" in the mix; hence there are more usable nutrients present in the meals.

It may seem more costly than grocery store brands but will in fact feed less of this kind of food and your cat will benefit health wise in the long run and you get to enjoy a bit of saving. Another benefit to premium dry cat food is there will be fewer poops to scoop out of your feline's litter box.

Essential Nutrients

It was mentioned a little earlier that a Russian Blue has no special nutritional requirements that are unusual or uncommon. The overall good health of the Blue will save you, the guardian, from spending for costly health care. This leaves you with a greater budget to provide top quality food.

The Russian Blue will essentially be meeting all its nutritional needs if given the proper provision of optimum pet food. Providing your RB with the right sort of high quality pet food will supply your feline all the vitamins, minerals and nutrients it would need to thrive and enjoy good health.

As your Russian Blue matures you will want to lessen its meal frequency from three meals to two meals a day, and possibly add more food each meal.

Foods and Ingredients to Avoid

Shun all food products which are labeled "by-products" and "meals". These foods come from questionable meat parts not fit for human consumption and regrettably end up in pet foods.

These questionable meat parts could be any unusable part of a cow, pork, or chicken, leftover from processing human food. These are likely to be chicken feet, beak, or legs, cow lungs, tongue, nose, hooves, tail, liver, or ear, and the list of possible contributors continue.

Additives are used to mask the inferiority of a food product. Many preservatives are carcinogens to humans and when used to produce pet food these preservatives limit bacteria growth or inhibit food oxidation.

Stay away from pet food products which have preservatives like BHT, sodium nitrate, nitrate, and BHA.

Artificial coloring are used to entice would be customers into making a purchase, but keep in mind, that these have no value in terms of nutrition, and may be the reason for allergic reactions in pets.

Remember that choosing the right sort of healthy food for your pet is your responsibility. Your pet will not bother how the food you serve looks, only how it tastes.

Types of Commercial Cat Foods

Premium dry cat food is possibly one of the best choices in food variants for your feline pet. It has a longer shelf life, it helps clean the teeth of your cat, and if of the optimum kind, it will provide the proper nourishment your Russian Blue needs.

High grade canned food, mixed in with a tiny amount of water, is also another pet food choice suitable to sustain all your Blues nutritional needs. This may not last as long outside the can and would need to be consumed within a short period of time but it will provide the proper nutrients your feline would need.

You may want to talk to your vet about alternative methods of feeding your Russian Blue feline. You can ask for a diet plan for the cat should you decides to feed it home cooked meals. Home cooked meals take more time to prepare and are largely determent of the quality of freshness of ingredients as well as thoughtful measurement. Keep in mind that you will need to measure out ingredients in accurate amounts to obtain the proper nutritional balance your feline will need.

Fresh Water

Cats aren't big drinkers and will most likely have to be regularly coaxed and reminded to take in fresh water. Water is very important to your feline pet as water helps replenish lost fluids spent during active play or physicality.

It has been observed that cats would favor drinking running water (or water from a fountain) to drinking from a bowl. No matter the choice they prefer, you should always leave out a fresh bowl of water for your feline to drink from when it is ready for a refreshing one.

Food Additives

The presence of food additives in any pet meal is to be questioned by any potential caregiver. You will need to develop uncanny skills of understanding food labels to confidently serve sound food to your pet.

There are food additives which are meant to enhance the quality and safety of the food. Then there are additives that are essentially unhealthy and are used as fillers and extenders to give the food volume and color.

Tips for Selecting a High-Quality Cat Food Brand

Stay away from the hype. Learn to read and decipher labels and study up on ingredients put into the mix of the food you serve your Blue.

Most high-end brands will boast of high quality ingredients in their products. It will be up to you to determine that by reading the label of the product. Products tagged as gourmet or premium are not actually bound to have different or better quality ingredients than other less costly, balanced and complete pet food products.

Foods boasting of a label reading "Natural" would contain ingredients gained only from animal, plant or mined sources. Natural foods cannot be overly processed nor should it contain synthetic ingredients like artificial flavors, preservatives, or coloring.

Organic pet foods are produced without the use of artificial fertilizers or conventional pesticides. These are free of contamination from human or industrial wastes and are not processed through ionizing radiation or food additives. If animal meats are involved in the production of foods, then the animals should have been raised sans the use of antibiotics or growth hormones and must have been fed a healthy diet. There are different levels of organic food. Whatever percentage a labels boasts is the percentage of organic ingredients used in the production of the food.

How (Much) To Feed Your Russian Blue

You may have to experiment a bit at the beginning to find the right kind of premium dry or canned foods your kitten will take a liking to, so purchase small amounts of cans and/or sacks at the beginning. You will be able to tell which ones they favor instantly by examining their bowls for how much left over there is. You will also be able to tell this by reading the cat's body language. You will have to look for other premium food options if your Russian Blue refuses to eat at all as this may lead to malnourishment.

To determine the amount of food you should give it each meal, experiment at the onset and give it two cups of premium dry cat food in a slow-feeding bowl. This dish is to be set out for only 30 minutes and should be eaten out of within that given time.

Once your feline has slow-fed for 30 minutes, measure the remaining dry food left in the feeding bowl and subtract that from the original amount of (2 cups of) food you set out and you will come up with the measure of food your feline is capable of eating each meal. Ideally, the "missing" amount of food would be the proper quantity to leave out for your cat for its succeeding meals.

You may have to repeat this procedure for about 2-3 days in order to get an accurate reading of the amount of food intake your kitten is able to consume.

You should start reducing the frequency of feeding your Russian Blue when it reaches 7 months. A more mature cat will not have to feed as often as when it was a kitten. However, it may be necessary to add a little more food for each meal when you lessen feeding frequency. Be mindful of the food you put out for the more mature kitten to prevent over feeding and food spoilage and wastage.

Chapter Seven: Showing Your Russian Blue Cat

Many cat aficionados find great joy in showing off their Russian Blue buddy for people to admire and get to know. This chapter is geared toward giving you, the reader, and information on the CFA Breeding Standards. Find out if your Russian Blue is eligible for registry with the Cat Fanciers Association and learn what requirements are sought out during the showing and judging of a Russian Blue at cat show events.

Whether show quality or otherwise, your Russian Blue cat will display outright affection and fondness to your longing kindness and repay you with undying loyalty and gratitude. You will surely enjoy the company and companionship of this clever and sometimes outspoken feline for many years to come now that you have come to understand what is needed from you as its guardian and lifelong friend.

CFA - Individual Registration

The application for registration to register your pet with the Cat Fanciers Association has to come from the breeder. You will want to get in touch with the breeder and ask for the Application for Registry which is also commonly referred to as a "blue slip".

You have to be aware that a reputable breeder may choose to withhold the release of the blue slip if you're buying agreement states that the feline has to be spayed or neutered before the registration paperwork is handed over to you. This is common practice for reputable breeders of pedigreed cats.

If the agreement is not met from your end, there is nothing the CFA can do until the terms of the sales contract is satisfied.

In order for the CFA to give registration to an individual feline in the absence of the standard application form, supporting documents must be provided accompanied by a request letter to CFA.

The documents needed are as follows; a pedigree or other supporting document, supplied by the breeder, which establishes the feline's eligibility to be registered under Cat Fanciers Association. The date of birth of the pet to be registered as well as its parent's CFA registration numbers. Additional information of whether the cat was bought with or without breeding rights is to be furnished as well.

Alternately, you may provide a copy of the written purchase agreement which states the conditions of the sale. This must be signed by all concerned parties. This agreement between the parties must indicate that CFA papers are to be provided. The birth date and identifying CFA registration numbers of the parents of the pet being registered must be included too whether the feline was bought with or without the right to breed.

Other supporting papers to include would be copies of canceled checks and receipts indicating full payment of the purchase. Copies of other documents indicating satisfaction in compliance of all other prerequisites to the release of the application form should also be provided by the breeder.

Upon receipt of these documents, the Central Office will get in touch with the breeder and ask for their cooperation and/or comments to speed up resolution of the matter.

In the event of submitting incomplete documents or information that is missing from these records, the Central Office will not be able to give you any assistance.

This would be a good time to remind you of clarifying details of your agreement with the breeder you will be working with. It is also a good time to figure out if you want your female feline to mate and breed later on. Determining these details at this early stage allows you to set expectations with your breeder, have all appropriate requirements transfer hands and documentation of all minor dealings (receipt, certifications, record of screening tests, etc.) filed away and ready at a moment's notice.

Plan on Breeding Your Russian Blue - What You Need to Know

In order for the CFA to register a feline with breeding privileges there must be a PIN written and present on the blue slip provided by the breeder.

This PIN is to be written in the PIN box enclosure of the Application for Registration or the blue slip. It is a 5-digit, random, computer-generated number which will be reflected only on the Certificate of Litter Registration given to the breeder.

For every litter registered there will be a different PIN assigned solely to that litter. Only the breeder of the said litter will have access to this PIN - the CFA will have no record of this.

If the cat were already registered with the CFA as a "Not For Breeding Cat," you will need to get in touch with the breeder to obtain the Litter PIN. You will need to write down the PIN on the registration certificate and bring it to the CFA with specific request to change the present NFB registration to a breeding cat. The fee for this correction is $15.00.

SHOWING YOUR RUSSIAN BLUE

(CAT STANDARD - Cat Fanciers Association)

HEAD and NECK...20

BODY TYPE... 20

COAT 20

COLOR... 20

EYE COLOR... 10

EYE SHAPE... 5

EARS.. 5

GENERAL: A feline of a good show specimen should be in optimum physical condition, its muscle tone should be firm, and it must be alert.

HEAD: A show grade Russian Blue feline's head is to display smooth, medium edge. It is neither long nor tapering nor should it be short and big. Muzzle of the feline is to show blunt, and part of the whole wedge, sans exaggerated pinch or break in whiskers. The top of the skull is to show long and flat when viewed from a profile. It is to gently descend to a little bit above the eyes as it continues at a slightly downward angle in a straight line to the tip of the nose. There is to be no visible nose stop or break. The length of the top-head must be greater than the length of the feline's nose. The face of the Russian Blue should display broad across the eyes due to its wide eye-set and thick, dense fur.

MUZZLE: The optimal show Russian Blue feline's muzzle should be a smooth, flowing wedge without pronounced whisker pads or whisker pinches.

EARS: The show feline's ears should be rather large and wide at the base. The tips of the feline's ears should be more pointed than it is rounded. The skin of the optimal show cat should be clear and translucent with very little inside furnishing. The outer part of the feline's ear should be scantily covered with short and very fine hair with the leather of the ear showing through. It must be set far apart as much from the sides as they are on the top of the head.

EYES: The eyes of a show quality Russian Blue is to be set wide apart and is to be aperture rounded in shape.

NECK: Its neck should be long and slender but must appear short because of the thick fur and the high placement of the shoulder blades.

NOSE: Its nose should be medium in length.

CHIN: The chin of a show quality Russian Blue should be perpendicular with the end of its nose and is level with under-chin. The chin should neither be receding nor should it be excessively massive.

BODY: The body of the show feline should have fine bones, long firm and muscular. It should be lithe and graceful in outline and carriage without the appearance of being tubular.

LEGS: The fore and hind legs of the feline are to be long and fine boned.

PAWS: The paws of the cat are to be small and slightly rounded. Its toes are to be counted five on each front paw and should count four on each hind leg.

TAIL: Its tail should be long but should be in proportion with its body. It should taper off from a moderately thick base.

COAT: Its coat is to be short, dense, plush and fine. The double coat is to stand out from to body due to thick density. It has to feel distinctly soft and silky to the touch.

DISQUALIFY: An immediate disqualification is called for a kinked or abnormal tail. Disqualified too is a count of incorrect number of toes. Any color other than blue is candidate for immediate disqualification and if the coat shows long rather than short.

Russian Blue Color Standard

COLOUR: The color of the Russian Blue is to be a bright blue throughout its body. Lighter shades of blue are preferred. Guard hairs are to display as distinctly silver-tipped giving the feline a silvery sheen and a lustrous appearance. A distinct contrast has to be noted between ground colors and tipping. It should be clear from tabby markings.

NOSE LEATHER: The nose leather of the Russian Blue is to be slate grey.

PAW PADS: Each paw pad of the show feline is to show a color of lavender pink or mauve.

EYE COLOUR: They eyes of the show Russian Blue is to be a vivid green.

There are no allowable outcross breeds for the Russian Blue Cat.

The Russian Blue Cat is covered with thick, dense fur known as a "double coat"; the undercoat of the fur is soft, downy and is equal in length with the evenly blue, silver tipped guard hairs - which when touched by light gives off a greater impression of the cat sporting a uniquely mesmerizing hue of silvery blue.

The two layers of its short, plush fur comes in subtle variations of blue-gray, which seems to shimmer when kissed by light. The bluish-gray color is the diluted expression of the black gene.

Now, as dilute genes are recessive ("d") and each of the parents will individually have a set of two recessive genes ("dd") two non-CPC Russian Blues will constantly sire and birth a blue cat.

The tail of the Russian Blue Cat, may have a few, very unnoticeable stripes which appear dull. The coat is plush, thick and soft to the touch.

The shimmering appearance of the coat is emitted by the silver tips of its fur. Its coat gives off the feel of the softest velvet when stroked. So dense is the coat of the Russian Blue that guardians of this breed have found great amusement in drawing patterns and "messages" on its dense coat only to delightfully discover that the pattern stays on the coat until it is smoothed over. This is another clever way of bonding with your cat.

The Russian Blue Cat's eyes are always a dark and vivid green and can be difficult to resist looking into once your Russian Blue locks sights with you. The hypnotic pair of bright green eyes beautifully contrasts its striking, blue-gray coat color and complements its overall appearance. It has the most adorable set of paws in hues ranging from pinkish lavender to/or mauve. Patches of white fur or eyes of yellow developed later in adulthood of the feline are seen to be flaws in show cats.

Russian Blues are not to be confused with British Blues - which are not a distinct breed, but rather a British Shorthair variety which also sports a blue coat. The British Shorthair sort is a breed which comes in an array or patterns and colors, and is not classified under the category of the Russian Blue Cat. Nor should Russian Blues be confused with the Korat or the Chartreux, which are naturally occurring in feline breeds of blue cats and somehow sharing similar traits.

Grooming and Hygiene

The Russian Blue is a relatively clean animal who manages to groom itself most of the time. This isn't to say that it will not need your help and assistance for other grooming needs it would require; but it is generally able to clean itself, thereby minimizing some of the work you, as future guardian will have to carry out.

Grooming your Russian Blue cat can also double as quality time spent with them if grooming is carried out in a non-invasive, non-threatening manner. Your feline will enjoy the feel of your hand running the length of its body, and you would've completed inspection of the soundness of its physique. You would have been able to inspect folds and tucked away areas of its body for any marring, clumping, bumps or lesions.

Chapter Eight: Breeding Your Russian Blue Cats

If you are interested in breeding your Russian Blue cat, this chapter will give you a wealth of information about the processes and phases of its breeding and you will also learn how to properly breed them on your own. You will also be given some grooming care tips so that you can ensure that your Russian Blue is clean, neat and presentable.

Russian Blue Cat Breeding Information

Before you think about breeding your Russian Blue, you will need to do proper research to ensure a successful outcome. It is imperative that you discuss this with your vet as your pet's physician can take measures to determine the sound health of your feline. Discuss the correct diet for pregnancy because some nutritional requirements will need to be increased.

If your cat is purebred, you will want to discuss potential health issues which may be inherited. Since the RB is a naturally occurring breed, the likelihood of it inheriting diseases from its parents is almost slim to none. But this doesn't mean you shouldn't discuss ethical methods of breeding.

Your vet is the best person to determine what problems are found to be common amongst the specific breed of your feline. Your vet is also the best person to deduce if your feline is a good candidate for breeding.

The temperament of the cat is an important factor to consider. A cat that is overly shy, highly nervous or anxious, or aggressive often makes poor parents and passes down these negative traits on to their offspring.

Mate selection for your feline should be carried out with thought, care and great consideration. Pick a mate that would best complement your pet's own temperament and its physical characteristics. Seek the advice of a seasoned breeder who can help you recognize your feline's strengths and weaknesses.

All purebreds recognized and acknowledged by different kennel clubs have set physical standards which need to be carefully considered because this is the goal of breeding kittens. You will need to study the standard guides of your cat and evaluate your feline against the allowed standard.

You should seek out a mate that would best complement and balance out your pet feline's temperament, structure, size and color.

Mating Behavior of Cats

Queens or female cats experience four hormonal cycles that dictate feline mating behavior. The whole head cycle lasts from 10 to 14 days. When the female cat is ready to mate she will display behaviors designed to attract a tom cat.

During this first stage (stage one), the female cat will begin to continuously rub its head and neck on anything it can rub up against. She may be vocal or quiet during this stage; she will appear restless and will consume more food than usual.

She will attract toms, but will be very selective and will likely refuse advances, opting for a period of increasing familiarity with the interested toms.

The queen may also urine mark in and around the house. A queen ripe for breeding and mating will go to great lengths to attract a suitable tom's attention. This is stage is short and may go unnoticed to the untrained eye.

If you want to prevent pregnancy you will want to get your feline spayed or at the very least keep it away from toms by keeping it indoors.

The second stage is called "heat"; this is when you will notice cat heat behavior. The signs mentioned earlier in stage one are all present but with greater intensity.

Your feline may be loud and vocal in its attempts to attract a likely tom partner. She will be more visibly affectionate and rub up against you more frequently. She will probably not want to be handled or picked up during this stage.

You will notice the female cat crouch with its forequarters pressed to the ground and the back hyper extended, exposing the vulva for the purpose of mating.

To test if your female cat is indeed in heat stroke its tail; if she raises her backside casting her tail off to the side, she is most likely in heat.

During the third stage of this period, if the female cat did not engage in sexual activity with a tom cat then the cycle will start again after this stage. During this period, the queen will not desire to mate with any tom cat.

The fourth stage lasts from November through to January, or a period of 90 days and this is thought to be due to shorter days.

Female Mating Behavior

When your female cat, or queen is ready to mate, she will get friendly with the Tom cat she finds to be a desirable partner. The cats will begin to explore each other's bodies not forgetting to include the face during this time of exploration. They will lick each other and set sights on each other's genitals.

This is how the female cat becomes aroused. Once arousal is established the queen will then assume the crouched position, tail to the side, exposing its vulva. This is seen when a female cat is ready to mate.

If the queen is not ready to be mounted, the mating process can turn out violent for the two cats. This occurs when the queen is in the middle of the first stage of the "heat" cycle and not yet ready or willing to welcome the tom. Queens have been known to bite and scratch at a tom to keep it at bay when the queen isn't quite ready yet. Queens are selective with toms they mate with and may refuse the advances of the tom you paired her up with.

Tom Cat Mounting Behavior

The tom will place his front paws on either side of the female cat as it takes grip of the female's neck using its teeth. He will move up and down using its back feet. The penis then penetrates the vulva and enters it until the tom ejaculates. The penis of the tom will stimulate the vagina of the female cat and will cause it to ovulate.

The queen will let out a shrill cry and will swiftly move away from the tom. The penis of the tom, with its sharp edges will likely cause pain to the female. The mating cats may repeat the procedure to make certain that the queen's ovulation has been successfully stimulated.

A female who had just copulated is not to be touched or moved until she has completed the last phase of the cat mating ritual which is the self-grooming process. This happens immediately after being mounted.

Chapter Nine: Keeping Your Russian Blue Cat Healthy

Some Russian Blues have been documented to live a long life of a maximum of 25 years. On an average, Russian Blues have a life expectancy of anywhere from 10-20 years. They are an almost perfect, health wise, as they historically have fewer health problems as compared to other breeds that are easily prone to inherited medical conditions or contract illnesses due to unsavory breeding methodology.

The robust RB has very little to no genetic issues and is not prone to illness like most other feline breeds. These quiet Blues are small to moderate in size, weighing an average of 2 to 7 kilograms, or 4.4 to 15.4 pounds, upon maturity - with males being typically bigger than females. The gestation period of a Russian Blue is about 64 days.

Common Health Problems

Below are some common health problems that Russian Blue cats are facing:

Cat Allergies

Based on personal accounts of Russian Blue Cat owners, evidence suggests that this breed may somewhat be better tolerated by individuals who suffer mild to moderate allergies.

The speculation is that the Russian Blue Cat may produce less glycoprotein (Fel d 1) which is one source of feline allergies. The denser coat of the Russian Blue may also keep more of the allergens closer to the cat's epidermis.

Glycoprotein is one of the culprits of cat allergies. The RBs likelihood to produce less of this does not mean they are more suitable to be companions to people with a history of being allergic to cats. Those individuals will still be likely to be affected by it, only to a much lesser degree for and for shorter periods of time.

Hypertrophic Cardiomyopathy

HCM or otherwise known as Hypertrophic Cardiomyopathy is a muscle disease in the heart wherein the heart muscles thicken and blocks arteries. Another common form of heart disease among cats is called DCM or Dilated Cardiomyopathy; it is a secondary disease that also damages the heart. HCM is caused by an overactive thyroid gland, while DCM is caused by a lack of amino acid Taurine. Common signs of this disease are rapid breathing, lethargy, and a poor appetite. Usually, symptoms don't appear, until it's too late. The cat has actually been suffering for several days to weeks before physical signs of this disease appear.

Most cats with cardiomyopathy have a heart murmur that can be detected during a wellness physical exam. It is highly recommended that you let your cat undergo through a genetic testing to detect a specific gene abnormality that may cause HCM and DCM.   Usually a specific diagnosis requires more advanced medical imaging. The best treatment is to detect it early that is why it is important to have your cat be screened at least twice a year.

Bonus Chapter

Beyond Russian Blue Cat

There is little factual information on the origins of the beautiful Russian Blue cat breed; however, the stories floating around to this day of its appearance are legendary.

Many surmise that the Russian Blue cat is a naturally occurring breed which originated from the Archangel Isles of Northern Russia, where long winters caused the development of the felines, plush, dense coat.

Talks of the RB cat originating from and produced by pet cats kept within the courts of Russian Czars still abound to this day. If it is to be assumed that the RB did come from the northern parts of Russia, it would have been likely shipped to the shores of England and other countries in Northern Europe in the mid-1860s by seafarers who would have traversed these channels.

The original Russian Blue Cat competed with all other blue cats of different breeds at the London Crystal Palace in 1875, and was the first recorded exhibition of this sort.

The Russian Blue cat was eventually given a separate class of its own for competition purposes when English and Scandinavian breeders started working to develop the bloodline foundation for the contemporary, more modern but, utterly traditional-looking, Russian Blue breed.

Russian Blues were imported to the United States in the early 1900s. It is to be remembered that it was not until after the end of the 2nd World War that breeders from North America started combining the European bloodlines to develop and produce cats with the distinct plush coats of the uniquely blue-gray hue, those engaging emerald colored peepers and the distinctive profile of the Russian Blue cat that seems to hint of a smile.

Since then and onward from the 1960s, the majestic Russian Blue began to gain popularity amongst feline breeds and has become a mainstay favorite at many cat shows and countless homes across the states and worldwide.

The lack of constant shedding is one of the favorite features mentioned by many Russian Blue cat guardians. The silky, dense short coat is plush and thick to the feel and seems to magically transform to an array of hues of blue and shades of grey with its every movement.

An even, stark, bright blue with each guard hair appearing to have been dipped in silver, gives the Russian Blue a silvery sheen and a lustrous, shimmering appearance of its coat. This unique breed is registered in one color only - blue - and only one coat length - short.

The eyes of the Russian Blue contrast its blue hue, with a stark and vivid, emerald green. Its head is shaped broad, of medium wedge with a noticeably flat top and a nose which is straight when inspected from profile.

Its large ears are seen wide at the base and set rather rakishly toward the sides of its head. This beautiful breed is considered a medium-sized feline who is fine-boned, firmly muscled and long.

Many years of thoughtful observation and selective breeding is what makes the Russian Blue more than any other blue-grey cat. Countless years of selective breeding and mindful registration of ancestry through pedigrees which only allow blue short-haired felines have resulted in a sort with an appearance of distinction and personality traits of which are unique to the RB are details which sets this breed apart from other felines - thereby making the RB a most affectionate companion and an entertaining addition to its guardians and friends.

Index

M

N

O

P

S

T

Photo Credits

Page 1 Photo by user milivanily via Pixabay.com, https://pixabay.com/en/cat-kitty-kitten-cute-home-lying-1512652/

Page 13 Photo by user Maslov_Slava via Pixabay.com, https://pixabay.com/en/cat-russian-blue-animal-cat-person-770261/

Page 25 Photo by user Sunny22 via Pixabay.com, https://pixabay.com/en/cat-animal-russian-blue-cat-762959/

Page 41 Photo by user Bartek2016 via Pixabay.com, https://pixabay.com/en/cat-russian-blue-eyes-near-1910266/

Page 56 Photo by user Brian Ramnath via Flickr.com, https://www.flickr.com/photos/sharpshoota/260223559/in/photolist

Page 65 Photo by user milivanily via Pixabay.com, https://pixabay.com/en/kitty-kitten-cat-domestic-cute-1512636/

Page 76 Photo by user Achatnia via Pixabay.com, https://pixabay.com/en/russian-blue-cat-tomcat-in-free-4855/

Page 89 Photo by user towoj via Pixabay.com, https://pixabay.com/en/cat-russian-blue-670548/

Page Photo 97 by user Sacha via Wikimedia Commons, https://commons.wikimedia.org/wiki/File:Russian_Blue_Cat _American_type.jpg

Page 102 Photo by user Own Work via Wikimedia Commons, https://commons.wikimedia.org/wiki/File:Russian_blue_cat.j pg

References

About the Russian Blue – CFA.org
<http://cfa.org/Breeds/BreedsKthruR/RussianBlue.aspx>

BREED PROFILE: Getting to Know the Russian Blue
<http://www.catscenterstage.com/breeds/russian-blue2.shtml>

Care and Feeding Guide – Platina Luna
<http://platinaluna.com/Care_and_Feeding_guide.htm>

Russian Blue - Wikipedia
<https://en.wikipedia.org/wiki/Russian_Blue>

Russian Blue Breed Standard – CFA.org
<http://cfa.org/Portals/0/documents/breeds/standards/russian.pdf>

Russian Blue – Purina.com
<https://www.purina.com/cats/cat-breeds/russian-blue>

Russian Blue Cat - Cattime.com
<http://cattime.com/cat-breeds/russian-blue>

Russian Blue Cats – Catster.com

<http://www.catster.com/cat-breeds/Russian_Blue>

Russian Blue Cat – Petmd.com

<http://www.petmd.com/cat/breeds/c_ct_russian_blue>

Russian Blue Cat: This Striking Robust Cat Could Be Your Companion for 15 to 20 Years – Mercola.com

<http://healthypets.mercola.com/sites/healthypets/archive/2015/02/21/russian-blue-cat.aspx>

Russian Blue/ Nebulung

<http://www.vetstreet.com/cats/russian-blue-nebelung>

Russian Blue Temperament and Personality – Russian Blue Love

<http://www.russianbluelove.com/russian-blue-temperament-and-personality/>

Feeding Baby
Cynthia Cherry
978-1941070000

Axolotl
Lolly Brown
978-0989658430

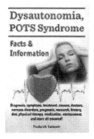

Dysautonomia, POTS
Syndrome
Frederick Earlstein
978-0989658485

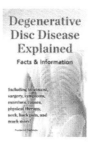

Degenerative Disc
Disease Explained
Frederick Earlstein
978-0989658485

Sinusitis, Hay Fever,
Allergic Rhinitis Explained
Frederick Earlstein
978-1941070024

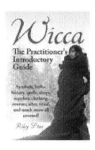

Wicca
Riley Star
978-1941070130

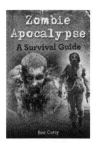

Zombie Apocalypse
Rex Cutty
978-1941070154

Capybara
Lolly Brown
978-1941070062

Eels As Pets
Lolly Brown
978-1941070167

Scabies and Lice Explained
Frederick Earlstein
978-1941070017

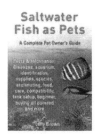

Saltwater Fish As Pets
Lolly Brown
978-0989658461

Torticollis Explained
Frederick Earlstein
978-1941070055

Kennel Cough
Lolly Brown
978-0989658409

Physiotherapist, Physical
Therapist
Christopher Wright
978-0989658492

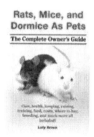

Rats, Mice, and Dormice
As Pets
Lolly Brown
978-1941070079

Wallaby and Wallaroo Care
Lolly Brown
978-1941070031

Bodybuilding Supplements
Explained
Jon Shelton
978-1941070239

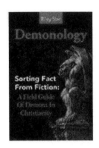

Demonology
Riley Star
978-19401070314

Pigeon Racing
Lolly Brown
978-1941070307

Dwarf Hamster
Lolly Brown
978-1941070390

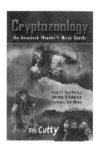

Cryptozoology
Rex Cutty
978-1941070406

Eye Strain
Frederick Earlstein
978-1941070369

Inez The Miniature Elephant
Asher Ray
978-1941070353

Vampire Apocalypse
Rex Cutty
978-1941070321

26577371R00070

Printed in Great Britain
by Amazon